UNLOCKING STUDENT POTENTIAL

How do I identify and activate student strengths?

Yvette
JACKSON | Veronica
MCDERMOTT

ASCD   Alexandria, VA USA

Website: www.ascd.org
E-mail: books@ascd.org

ASCD | arias™
www.ascdarias.org

Printed in the United States of America. Cover art © 2015 by ASCD. ASCD publications present a variety of viewpoints. The views expressed or implied in this book should not be interpreted as official positions of the Association.

ASCD LEARN TEACH LEAD® and ASCD ARIAS™ are trademarks owned by ASCD and may not be used without permission. All other referenced trademarks are the property of their respective owners.

PAPERBACK ISBN: 978-1-4166-2115-7   ASCD product # SF115057

Also available as an e-book (see Books in Print for the ISBNs).

Library of Congress Cataloging-in-Publication Data

Jackson, Yvette.
  Unlocking student potential : how do I identify and activate student strengths? / Yvette Jackson, Veronica McDermott.
    pages cm
  Includes bibliographical references.
  ISBN 978-1-4166-2115-7 (Paperback : alk. paper) 1. Learning ability-
-Identification. 2. Motivation in education. I. McDermott, Veronica.
II. Title.
  LB1134.J37 2015
  370.15'23--dc23
                          2015025475
───
24 23 22 21 20 19 18 17 16 15   1 2 3 4 5 6 7 8 9 10

UNLOCKING STUDENT POTENTIAL

How do I identify and activate student strengths?

Want to earn a free ASCD Arias e-book?
Your opinion counts! Please take 2–3 minutes to give
us your feedback on this publication. All survey
respondents will be entered into a drawing to
win an ASCD Arias e-book.

Please visit
www.ascd.org/ariasfeedback

Thank you!

Starting from Strengths

Who among us wants to be reminded, yet again, of the negative, of our shortcomings, of long-standing and seemingly intractable failure? Education policy has long asked educators to mine for what is wrong with students, to search for their deficits, to pinpoint where they fall short of arbitrary standards devoid of context, and to find ways to *remediate* their performance.

Our orientation is totally opposite. We posit that if you (regardless of your role) start with strengths, you have the capacity to unlock the potential of every student—and teacher—in your school. The real achievement gap is not one that highlights the distance between the performance of students of different races and a set of normative achievement levels but between individual performance and individual potential (Jackson, 2011).

As lifelong educators serving students in the public schools of New York State and New York City, we have first-hand experience of the brilliance of our underachieving students and the systems that often fail them. Our work with the National Urban Alliance (NUA) has taken us to U.S. schools of every kind (urban, rural, suburban) where we have met educators like you who are eager to cultivate potential. And they love the idea that you can start with something simple:

identifying and activating student strengths. Although many of the examples provided are from middle schools, they can be modified for all grade levels and can be used by teachers; school, department, and district leaders; coaches; and school counselors.

This book draws upon our experiences working in schools repeatedly labeled as underachieving that are transforming themselves through the implementation of the *Pedagogy of Confidence*® (Jackson, 2011), an approach designed to help all students become self-directed learners rather than school-dependent ones. The foundation of the Pedagogy of Confidence is a set of seven interrelated High Operational Practices™:

- Identifying and activating student strengths
- Building relationships
- Eliciting high intellectual performance
- Providing enrichment
- Integrating prerequisites for academic learning
- Situating learning in the lives of students
- Amplifying student voice (Jackson, 2011, p. 89)

"Identifying and activating student strengths" is deliberately listed first, because it has been neglected for so long as a practice for reversing underachievement and increasing learning (Jackson, 2011). Additionally, starting from strengths kick-starts a new, positive, and powerful way of learning, teaching, and being; a way in which students and teachers are motivated by the affirmation of their strengths and their potential.

Why Shine the Spotlight on Strengths?

Jettisoning the deficit model and replacing it with one that starts from student strengths is a no-cost, highly effective, nontraditional way of addressing persistent underachievement. Sadly, as a 2014 Gallup poll suggests, paying attention to strengths is not something U.S. schools do very well.

What students say. The 20-question Gallup student poll measures three elements—hope, engagement, and well-being—that predict student academic success and future employment. The survey is given to students in grades 5–12 whose buildings have opted to be part of the poll. As such, it is a selective sampling of how students think about hope, engagement, and well-being.

The engagement survey contains three questions that directly address strengths:

- At this school, I have the opportunity to do what I do best every day.
- In the last seven days, I have received recognition or praise for doing good schoolwork.
- My school is committed to building the strengths of each student.

These three questions received the lowest average score of all the survey questions. Further, the scores declined as students moved up in grade level.

These results suggest that capitalizing on strengths is not part of our pedagogical investment strategy and becomes even less of a focus as students progress through school. If the scores on these questions went up each year, building on what was developed the year before, imagine how different high school classes would look and feel; how involved and enthusiastic high school graduates would be; what would happen to dropout rates; what a rewarding experience teaching high school seniors would be.

What adults say. Adults, too, know when their strengths are being used and when they are not. Its impact on job satisfaction and productivity is huge. Workplace studies indicate that when leadership focuses on an employee's strengths, the odds that the employee will be engaged, be productive, and feel a sense of well-being increases eightfold compared to when leaders fail to focus on the strengths of their employees (Rath & Conchie, 2008).

The strengths spiral. Early self-awareness of strengths has long-lasting effects. Students who are aware of their strengths and know how to employ them strategically generally meet with success. Success breeds success. Our job as educators is to provide opportunities for all students to benefit from this cumulative advantage.

Standards

Focusing on strengths has the power to unlock student—and teacher—potential. The big question is how do schools transition from deficit thinking to strengths thinking. When it comes to poking holes in the deficit narrative about underperforming students, we have found that the following *what if* exercise works wonders.

Imagine this: At your next foray into data mining or the next grade level, department, or faculty meeting, you and your colleagues focus on a simple question, one we always use when we meet a faculty for the first time: What are the **strengths** of our underachieving students?

You may want to try this yourself. What words would you choose? Creative? Resilient? Verbal? Honest? Loyal? Relationship-Oriented? Multilingual? Tenacious? Media Savvy? Do your underachieving students also display the ability to problem solve, meet multiple demands, or take on adult responsibilities? In other words, are they able to judge, analyze, compare, contrast, and synthesize? These abilities represent important cognitive skills, used by anyone in the course of learning new information.

These abilities also closely align with many of the descriptors of college and career readiness found in the Common Core State Standards, as well as state and district goals. A quick look at the desired outcomes of the English and mathematics goals of the Common Core standards proves this point. As defined in the standards (National Governors Association Center for Best Practices & Council of Chief State School Officers, 2010), students who are college and career ready do the following:

In English they

- Demonstrate independence.
- Build strong content knowledge.
- Respond to varying demands of audience, task, purpose, and discipline.
- Comprehend and critique.
- Value evidence.
- Use technology and digital media.
- Understand other perspectives and cultures.

In mathematics they

- Make sense of problems and persevere in solving them.
- Reason abstractly and quantitatively.
- Construct viable arguments and critique the reasoning of others.
- Model.
- Use appropriate tools strategically.
- Attend to precision.
- Look for and make use of structure.
- Look for and express regularity in repeated reasoning.

An interesting exercise is to make explicit the ways in which your underachieving students demonstrate these goals, often in out-of-school settings. Do they demonstrate independence? Do they have the ability to comprehend deeply? How about their skills in the use of technology and digital media? When and how do they make sense of problems and persevere? Can they construct viable arguments and critique the reasoning of others? In other words, your underachieving students possess many of the prerequisite cognitive skills demanded by the standards.

The question for educators is how do you tap into these skills that are often demonstrated in out-of-school or nonacademic settings so that students are aware of their strengths, inclined to employ them in school-oriented activities, and strategic in their ability to apply them with competence and confidence for self-directed learning, self-actualization, and making personal contributions?

What Science Says About Identifying and Activating Strengths

Whenever we shepherd a group of educators through strengths-identifying activities, we have the privilege of observing the way the energy in the room changes. Teachers—many of whom work in schools in their district or state deemed to be "low performing"—become animated. They smile. They laugh. Their eyes open, literally and figuratively. They see their students through the powerful lens of potential, capacity, and possibility. Their task as educators seems less daunting, maybe even joyful.

When teachers recognize and activate student strengths, the students themselves are also transformed. They are better prepared to do what they were born to do: learn. Students begin to believe in themselves as capable, valued, and respected. They define themselves as learners. They are willing to invest and engage in school. They perform better. They crave and enjoy academic challenge, and they delight in outdoing themselves.

There is a neurobiological reason for these positive feelings teachers and students experience. When you identify students' strengths, their innate potential is confirmed for you and for them. This confirmation expands both your belief in their ability and motivation to excel and in your belief in your ability to elicit and nurture their potential and abilities. It also expands your students' beliefs in their own potential. For both teachers and students, this acknowledgment of strengths activates the "glow" of competence and confidence—the neurological response from the stimulation they begin to experience (Jackson, 2011, p. 9; Jensen, 1998).

Both cognitive science, the interdisciplinary scientific study of the mind and its processes, and neuroscience, the science of the nervous system which makes up one aspect of cognitive science, have revealed some exciting and useful information about how the brain receives, processes, and retrieves information.

Confidence acquired from competence causes us to become intensely stimulated. This stimulation causes a burning of glucose, which results in our brain "glowing" from the energy of the glucose that is consumed. The stimulation is actually acting like a brain "nutrient," making us feel stronger. For teachers, demonstrations of student learning and success resulting from our teaching serve as feedback to us about our choices. This feedback is a great asset, because it fuels us with both a deep sense of competence and a sense of being valued. This sense of competence and being valued releases neurotransmitters of pleasure—endorphins—which help us enjoy our work more. When feelings of competence are increased, fewer catecholamines (the body's natural chemical response to stress) are released. (Jackson, 2011, p. 9)

For students, affirmation of their strengths is feedback to them about their learning and potential. When you highlight your underachieving students' strengths—and you and your students experience the "glow" that accompanies such an exercise—the culture of the school changes. School takes on the sparkle of a place where lives can be transformed and differences are the stuff of celebration. It embodies and cultivates "teaching, learning, and other miracles," not for material success, but as part of what Grace Feuerverger calls "a sacred life journey, a quest toward liberation" (2007, p. 1).

Once you change the way you look at your underachieving students, it becomes impossible to see them through a deficit lens. As one teacher put it, "You cannot *un-see* what you have seen." The same is true for the students themselves. By highlighting and affirming your students' strengths and the positive ways in which this knowledge makes you and your students feel, you have taken the first step toward transforming learning outcomes and eradicating what we have termed the crime of squandered potential (Jackson & McDermott, 2012).

If you are interested in flipping the script on student underachievement by shifting the focus from one of mining for deficits to one of identifying and activating student strengths, you have clearly identified your *intention*. The question, then, is what do you need to pay *attention* to in order to reap the benefits of a focus on strengths? The rest of this book is designed to provide you with the understandings, strategies, and examples to help you apply a strength-based approach to learning and teaching in your school or classroom.

What Are Strengths and How Do They Work?

Strengths are the outgrowth of interests activated by exposure and practice. Identifying and activating student strengths inspires students' belief in their thinking and potential. It encourages investment in learning and ownership of the process of self-actualization (Jackson, 2011).

For many students, especially younger students and those conditioned to think of themselves negatively, some priming needs to be done to help them recognize what strengths are. Young students in particular equate strengths with muscle, sinew, and brawn. A little guidance helps them to understand that when you are talking about strengths you mean qualities such as strength of character, mental functions, and habits of mind or dispositions, and not physical strength.

Several years ago the entire 6th grade of a school that had the dubious distinction of having been labeled a school in need of improvement years before the enactment of No Child Left Behind wrote, produced, and narrated a 30-minute radio show as part of a StudentVoice/NUA project entitled *Strong Voices; Strong Futures* (Jackson & McDermott, 2012, p. 127; McDermott, 2010). The final production contained radio diaries highlighting personal strengths, including an interview with a child battling cancer; a feature interview with a teacher about a strategy that builds on strengths; and sound bites of individuals' comments about strengths, whether they were teachers, custodians, or family members who happened to be visiting during the taping. The radio show also included a bilingual radio play, professional sounding opening and closing, sound effects, and "stringers" to bridge between segments.

The entire project was strengths-based. Prior to the production week, students engaged in conversations around different kinds of character traits and talents. After exploring the notion that strengths meant much more than physical prowess, students were ready for a challenge. Presented with evocative photographs of four different animals engaged in a variety of activities, their task was to select the photo that represented one of their strengths and explain how that photo represented that strength.

Their answers were nothing short of astounding. Their ability to think metaphorically and explain their choices with minute details gleaned from the photographs and honest introspection was inspiring. The interest and delight in hearing each other's interpretations was matched only by their intense and genuine appreciation of the different interpretations provided by their schoolmates. They described themselves with a rich vocabulary of words: *courageous, inventive, caring, committed, intelligent, creative, competent, confident, dependable, supportive, dedicated,* and *adventurous.*

A radio producer introduced them to the various job titles and tasks associated with putting a radio show together. Based upon these descriptions, students completed an application indicating their top three choices and the specific strengths they possessed that would make them the ideal candidate for their preferred job.

Several points are worth making here.

- Students demonstrated deep insight into their character and their strengths. Students' job choices were not denied because of a mismatch between their self-identified strengths and the skills required by the positions.

- Students appreciated the range of strengths exhibited by their classmates. They supported and accepted each other. During the taping of the radio play they wrote, no one commented on the fact that one student needed his one-on-one aide to assist him with his part. Indeed, without prompting, students consistently praised each other's efforts.
- All students threw themselves into their different tasks with enthusiasm, excitement, and a desire to do the best job they could. They were not discouraged by multiple retakes, involved directions, or learning to use unfamiliar professional recording equipment.
- They all demonstrated outstanding aptitude, laser sharp focus, and deep commitment to the tasks at hand. Danny's post-assignment declaration, "I feel like a CEO!", is evidence of the pride most students felt in their accomplishments (McDermott, 2010). Alex's postproduction reflection was also telling: "When Ms. A told us we were going to create a radio show, I thought it was stupid. Now I know it would have been stupid if I was not part of it."

The plan for the radio show deliberately provided opportunities for students to uncover their interests and strengths. They were exposed to ways of employing their interests and strengths in novel ways. (Before the project, most students had never heard a radio program of the type they produced.) They had multiple opportunities to practice and rehearse before their performances were committed to tape.

"A focus on strengths animates intellectual capacity when students are able to act on their strengths by applying them and creating with them independently or interdependently (Renzulli, 1975; Renzulli & Reis, 2007)" (Jackson, 2011, p. 105). Repeated and differentiated opportunities to employ aptitudes, abilities, competencies, and talents are hallmarks of education programs designed for so-called gifted and talented students. Students in schools who, by virtue of their family circumstances, live in a pocket of deep poverty and attend a school persistently labeled a failure, typically have few opportunities to engage in enrichment activities where they are free to employ their aptitudes, abilities, competencies, and talents. Fortunately for the 60 6th graders who produced the radio show, they had a principal and staff who eagerly embraced the Pedagogy of Confidence, and therefore these students had the opportunity to experience learning and teaching in a different form.

All students possess unique aptitudes, abilities, competencies, and talents. Opportunities to develop and display strengths must not be rationed and only given to those students identified as gifted and talented (Jackson, 2011). Instead, opportunities to develop and display strengths must be built into the fabric of learning and teaching every day for *every* student.

How Does Identifying and Activating Strengths Mitigate Underperformance?

Young children internalize self-image and their place in society at a very early age. One of the most telling examples of this can be found in the 2005 documentary, *A Girl Like Me* (www.youtube.com/watch?v=YWyI77Yh1Gg) produced by then 16-year-old Kiri Davis. Among other things, this seven-minute video recreates the study conducted by Kenneth Clark in the 1940s, in which African American children were asked to choose between black and white dolls. The majority of the children selected white dolls. Some 60 years later, Kiri repeated the experiment and vividly caught on tape these preschool children's struggles with self-image. When asked to select the "nice," "pretty," or "good" doll, 15 of the 21 children selected the white doll.

Left unchecked—or worse, deepened through years of negative school experiences—this negative self-image solidifies. By middle school, students who have rarely seen themselves as worthy, strong, and full of assets are stymied when asked to identify their strengths. They need prodding and prompting. They require reminders of their merit.

This is what happened in Newark, New Jersey, when Yvette was working with a group of middle schoolers. Initially, none of the students could name strengths they possess. Only after Yvette primed each one with a specific strength she had noticed were they able to complete the task. Once they got going, however, they were able to identify multiple strengths of their own and other students. That's the good news: Identifying strengths is contagious. Just talking about your strengths leads to feel-good emotions, which are the effect of endorphins and dopamine. They mitigate the deleterious effect negative experiences have on the brain and learning (Jackson, 2011, p. 92).

The brain responds to the environment. The more opportunities you have to cultivate and employ your strengths, the more likely you are to develop the self-esteem that fuels your motivation to exhibit these strengths more and more frequently, thus leading to a cycle of success (Anderson, 2005). And the brain becomes more efficient with practice. Experience and practice grow neurons. More neurons lead to more efficient processing of information (Holloway, 2003). Thus repeatedly employing strengths builds stronger brain circuitry leading to faster, more efficient learning.

Eric Jensen (2005, p. 69) lists 11 ways in which emotions affect learning. Among other things he indicates that emotions help orchestrate attentional priorities, support either persistence or retreat, help us make meaning, provide incentives, and allow learners to enjoy and celebrate success. Emotions are one of several learning systems that are a natural part of the way the brain operates during learning situations (Costa & Kallick, 2014).

A simple experiment provides powerful testimony to the impact identifying strengths has on learning. Psychologists from Yale University discovered that prior to taking a mathematics test, those students who completed a simple 15-minute assignment in which they wrote affirmations about their strengths to elicit positive identity and self-integrity increased their performance and reduced the racial achievement gap in mathematics by 40 percent. As the researchers explained, school settings in general, and testing situations in particular, are often stressful for students.

African American students, they further explained, can be even more threatened in testing situations due to a history of negative stereotypes about how their group performs in particular settings (Cohen, Garcia, Apfel, & Master, 2006). These stereotype threats (Steele & Aronson, 2005) can be counteracted when students are given opportunities to express their values and abilities.

Teachers familiar with these findings now know that they are key to student outcomes. How they construct lessons, shape the culture of their classroom, and orient themselves to their students can have significant positive outcomes on how and what their students learn.

Our job, then, is twofold. We need to reframe the way we view our underperforming students, and we need to provide them with opportunities to shine a spotlight on their strengths. As you move from a deficit view to a strengths-based view, how you see your students and how they see themselves changes. There is nothing more exciting than to see students independently and continuously employing their strengths in an ever-widening range of situations.

AIM High: A Protocol to Shine the Spotlight on Strengths

In our previous book, *Aim High, Achieve More*, we introduced a simple way to jumpstart and sustain the transformation process, which we summarized in the acronym AIM: affirm, inspire, and mediate (Jackson & McDermott, 2012). Individual teachers, groups of like-minded educators, and entire schools can benefit from applying the three-step process to isolate in concrete terms what they need to pay attention to in order to achieve the intended outcome. Here is how it works.

Affirm the current reality. How, in fact, are strengths currently identified and activated in your school or classroom?

To accurately determine the current reality of strengths identification and activation, first determine what one might see, hear, or experience in a strengths-saturated learning environment. We find it helpful to create a rubric that captures three levels of implementation: Barely Present, Emerging, and Soundly in Place.

After isolating and defining key elements of strengths-based learning, you are ready to determine where your school or classroom is on the continuum.

Inspire yourself to move to the next level of practice. Knowing where you are is second in importance to determining where you want to be. The rubric helps to point the way, to inspire you to move to the next level of practice.

Mediate to achieve your goal. *Mediation* is the term the celebrated cognitive psychologist Feuerstein used to describe activities and actions that support movement to the next level of practice. Mediation can take many forms from personally driven change to change that is supported by others (Feuerstein, 1979). In this phase, consider what you may have to change, learn about, or get support for in order to move along the continuum. We find that working with others drives mediation by providing much needed support, feedback, and new ideas.

The following scenario demonstrates how one organization progressed through the steps of affirmation, inspiration, and mediation to move their organization to the next level of practice.

Affirmation: At the start of the 2014 school year, a group of educators who work with a marginalized and largely underachieving group of students considered the following question: *What would students, staff, family members, and community members see, feel, hear, and do if their strengths were identified and activated?*

Educators worked in small groups to consider what the practice would look and feel like if it was barely present, emerging, or soundly in place. They recorded their thoughts on a Tree Map, one of eight Thinking Maps® (Hyerle, 2004). (Thinking Maps are tools to help students identify patterns and relationships. For more information, visit www.thinkingmaps.com.) Figure 1 shows the picture that emerged by combining all of the group's ideas.

It is interesting to note the number of entries that deal with emotions: *feel safe, feel encouraged,* and *feel positive self-esteem*. Clearly these educators realized the enormous role feelings and emotions play in learning and teaching.

Although the group felt that they created a positive and supportive learning atmosphere, they realized that they could more consistently and deliberately use language to underscore their belief that the students are highly capable and strengths-endowed.

Inspiration: Before embarking on an examination of the language of their organization, they sought inspiration.

FIGURE 1: Identify and Activate Student Strengths Tree Map

Identify and Activate Student Strengths

Barely Present

Students

- Do what they're told
- No flexibility in programming
- Feel anxious/inadequate
- Hear negative language
- Feel an indifference toward the program
- Would not see a reflection of themselves in the classroom/building; nothing personalized

Emerging

Students

- Feel encouraged
- Feel comfortable
- Feel accepted
- Feel supported
- Willingly participate
- Make greater effort
- Hear more positive language
- Choose activities & give feedback
- See students artwork/creative pieces
- Take risks (less shutting down)
- Ask questions
- OK to make mistake

Soundly in Place

Students

- Positively engaged students
- Feel ownership of the space
- See success academically and in all areas
- Strong relationships with staff
- Feel positive self-esteem
- Happy with themselves
- Feel confident
- Designing and Leading program
- Feel safe to be themselves
- Safe place to fall
- Feel cared for

Adapted from Hyerle, 2004

Working with a facilitator, they attempted to understand more deeply the impact of language on the psyche.

They examined a wide range of artifacts, including items displayed in trophy boxes in board of education conference rooms to bulletin boards in kindergarten classrooms. One example from a 5th grade classroom particularly resonated with them. This teacher-generated list of class rules—complete with colorful lettering and illustrations—greeted the students at the start of the school year:

Class Rules

1. No bullying
2. Indoor voices
3. Ask permission
4. Raise hand
5. Listen
6. No running
7. No foul language
8. No disrespect
9. Work hard
10. Have fun!!!

The workshop participants concluded the following about the message behind the message:

- Greeting students with a list of *rules* implies that students are unruly and thus reinforces a negative self-perception.
- By listing specifics like No Foul Language, No Disrespect, and Work Hard, the negative is further reinforced with the implication that these 5th graders

are expected to use foul language, will likely not show respect, and probably will not work hard.

- Although establishing well-managed, well-functioning learning environments is a worthy goal, without careful analysis of how that is done and the words used by adults, organizations can inadvertently give negative messages and miss attention to the role they play in affecting the environment.
- The poster of class rules did little to support their goal of providing students with a consistent and powerful message that they are highly capable, strengths-endowed students.

Mediation: The group also came up with three ways to mediate the examples. The first was to use a different title. Something like Ways We Work Together implies that students know how to work together, value working together, and can describe what it looks like. Second, they felt strongly that students and teachers should develop the list together. Third, they suggested that the list be a living document.

Continuing with the notion that word choice can inadvertently send a negative message, they decided to critically analyze and mediate one of their in-house documents, a flyer to advertise a summer high school transition program. This series of sessions is designed to smooth the sometimes anxious transition from elementary school to secondary school.

Below is the list of workshop titles they traditionally run, and in fact had just completed:

- What to Expect in High School and How to Be Safe

- Conflict Resolution
- Dealing with Competition and Anxiety
- How to Ask for Help

Their critical analysis of these workshop titles was eye opening. They determined that the message was that high school is not safe; that there will be conflicts, competition, and anxiety; and that their students will need help. Participants self-mediated and rewrote the titles to be affirming, positive, and reflective of the belief in their students as capable. For example, How to Ask for Help became Putting Your Problem-Solving Abilities to Work.

Inspired by the notion that they can and should monitor the language used in printed and oral communication, they set up a plan to monitor each other and deliberately look at all of their printed material to ensure that there is a consistent message that students are capable, have potential, and have strengths that they can activate and employ in any given situation.

"Gifting" All Students with an Emphasis on Strengths

Reuven Feuerstein has a simple formula for changing outcomes: Change the inputs, and the outcomes change accordingly (Feuerstein, 1979; Feuerstein, Feuerstein, & Falik, 2010).

In other words, if your **intention** is to encourage *all* students to cultivate and employ their strengths, then you need to pay **attention** to the ways in which you explicitly set up opportunities for *all* students to discover and use their strengths. Schools know how to do this. Historically, they have organized gifted and talented programs around a strengths-based approach. The goal is to find ways to employ the same organizing principles for all students. To do so requires rethinking the beliefs, practices, and structures that underlie learning and teaching activities in your school or classroom.

It Begins with Belief

If you believe that your underachieving students have strengths, you will have higher expectations for them and undoubtedly "gift" them with opportunities to demonstrate those strengths to meet these higher expectations (Jackson, 2011). That is exactly what happens in traditional gifted and talented programs. The starting off point is that so-called gifted and talented students have strengths in one or more preordained areas (Renzulli, 1978, 1998). Their teachers are skilled in ways to draw out and build upon these capacities, talents, or aptitudes, and they are primed to expect great things from students labeled gifted and talented. No one seems to see as a deficit the fact that most gifted and talented individuals do not manifest their giftedness all the time nor in every area of their lives, a sobering thought that Joseph Renzulli, among others, has made clear.

So let's begin with the belief that all students have strengths (gifts) upon which you can and should build.

Aligning Beliefs, Practices, and Structures for a Different Outcome

If you begin with the belief that all of your students have strengths upon which you can build, your practices and structures will change, leading to different outcomes (Jackson, 2011). Underachieving students blossom when given opportunities to demonstrate learning connected to their personal experiences or interests. They become animated when allowed to grapple with complex, real world problems that require insight and a critical eye. Students are engaged when teachers provide alternative ways of presenting information and give them choice in the kinds of activities they are asked to do to demonstrate their knowledge.

Starting the Year Off by Identifying Strengths

Starting the year off with a focus on strengths is a powerful morale booster. Here are several suggestions for ways to identify strengths at the beginning of the year.

Alliterative Introductions

When we begin a professional learning experience we often start with a community builder we call Alliterative Introductions. It is a very quick and enjoyable activity that teachers love to replicate and expand upon with their students. The bonus is that students love it!

Alliteration is when two or more words in close proximity to each other begin with the same sound. In Alliterative Introductions, participants introduce themselves by pairing their first name with an adjective that describes them, has a positive connotation, and begins with the same sound as their first name. Yvette often uses Youthful Yvette. Veronica always describes herself as Vivacious Veronica.

What makes the introductions an inviting challenge is that each person introduces all of the people who have already introduced themselves BEFORE they get to make their personal introduction. We use the following speaking frame: *This is Jolly Jim, Bubbly Barbara, Wonderful Juan. I am Persistent Petronella.*

We have yet to lead this activity without playful cheating and lots of laughter as people at the end of the line struggle to remember the monikers of those who came before. Without much effort students internalize what alliteration means, which often primes them for other types of word play.

Sometimes students can use some help in coming up with adjectives. The English Club, a website devoted to helping people learn English, provides a list of 100 positive adjectives that describe personalities: www.englishclub.com/vocabulary/adjectives-personality-positive.htm. A more extensive list of adjectives can be found at Enchanted Learning: www.enchantedlearning.com/wordlist/adjectives-forpeople.shtml. However, this list includes adjectives of a positive and negative nature.

Providing students with word banks is a powerful and engaging way of building students' vocabularies. It also allows students a chance to employ strengths such as the abilities to cooperate and employ background knowledge. Students who know the meaning of particular adjectives enjoy explaining the meaning of these words to their peers. Students whose first language is other than English often employ their first language to figure out the meanings of different words and experience the joy of seeing the benefit of being multilingual.

Sometimes unexpected strengths can be revealed through activities such as Alliterative Introductions, as the following anecdote makes clear.

One day Veronica was using Alliterative Introductions with a group of 5th and 6th grade students labeled under-achieving. The students were meeting a group of volunteer scientists, mathematicians, and engineers who were part of a Saturday science and math exploration program. As the 25 students and adults went around the room introducing each other and themselves, the level of enjoyment—and play-ful cheating—kept growing. Veronica, as usual, planned to introduce herself as Vivacious Veronica. Standing next to her was Tamara, who introduced herself as Tenacious Tamara. *Vivacious* and *tenacious* are two vocabulary words that are rarely found in the lexicon of 5th and 6th graders, especially those labeled underachieving.

The following week, one of the students, Josiah, who was long believed to be a struggling student, excitedly asked if they were going to play "that name game again." When told no, he appeared visibly disappointed. "Why did you ask?" Veronica questioned him. "Because I memorized all of them," Josiah said, and then proceeded to point to where each student and volunteer was standing the week before. He accurately recalled all of their names and adjectives, including Vivacious Veronica and Tenacious Tamara! Clearly, Alliterative Introductions identified a strength no one knew Josiah possessed, an extraordinary memory.

Using Alliterative Introductions to Create a Taxonomy of Strengths

Teachers often build upon this activity by posting the Alliterative Introductions using an ABC Taxonomy in which all of the students' names and their accompanying adjectives are listed.

A taxonomy is simply a list of words related to a particular topic or subject area. The purpose of an ABC Taxonomy is to make the list of words more accessible and generative by organizing the words alphabetically (Rothstein, Rothstein, & Lauber, 2006). In the end, the words generated by every member of the class become usable by all, because as Evelyn Rothstein often says, "Words are free."

Taxonomy of Strengths

A. artistic Anisha, altruistic Ahmed	N.
B. brainy Bianca	O. optimistic Olivia
C. caring Carmen	P. positive Pedro
D. dedicated Daquan	Q.
E.	R. responsible Ricardo

F. funny Fernando	S. sophisticated Sofia
G. giving Gloria	T. talented Tanesha
H. humble Henry	U. understanding Ushana
I. intellectual Ivan	V. vivacious Vivian
J. jubilant Jamaar	W.
K. kind Kathy	X.
L. loving Lucas	Y.
M. multilingual Miguel	Z.

The Taxonomy of Strengths serves many purposes and can be expanded upon in many ways across all grade levels. Here are several ideas that teachers have used:

- Teachers encourage students to supply examples of how they manifest the adjectives they choose. In this way, they are preparing them for the demands of the Common Core standards, which often ask students to provide details, examples, and arguments to support their answers.
- In their study of literature, social studies, and current events, students remain on the lookout for evidence of any of the adjectives that appear on the Taxonomy of Strengths and the specific way in which the characteristic is demonstrated. What often emerges for students is an understanding that literature frequently reflects life and that history is full of individuals and groups of people who have often used their best qualities to deal with trying situations, everyday occurrences, and extraordinary happenings.

By thinking through and discussing different traits, students come to know more profoundly what it means to be, for example, *responsible* or *resourceful* or *resilient*. In other words, they deepen their understanding of these often abstract concepts.

- Another vocabulary building variation of this activity is to have students create a list of synonyms for their original list of adjectives. Students are encouraged to use this enhanced adjective list in their writing and speaking.

Strengths Audits

Starting from strengths means starting the school year off deliberately, intentionally, and explicitly mining for strengths. For many schools, this means conducting a strengths audit during the first days of school. A Strengths Audit, unlike Alliterative Introductions, requires deeper reflection.

A Strengths Audit begins as a self-reflection activity in which students and teachers indicate their strengths. These audits can be free form, in which participants brainstorm their strengths, or they can be guided. We often use a Circle Map, one of the Thinking Maps (Hyerle, 2004), to brainstorm ideas to define a concept or a theme.

In Figure 2, the example on the left invites participants to brainstorm the strengths that they self-identify. In the Circle Map on the right, they are guided to consider the strengths they exhibit in different categories of activities. Many schools engage teachers in these activities prior to completing them with their students.

FIGURE 2: **Circle Maps for Capturing Self-Identified Strengths**

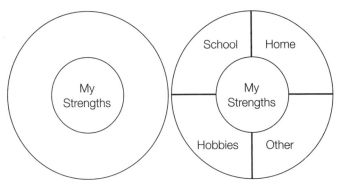

Adapted from Hyerle, 2004

Strengths Audits can also be used

- **For reflection.** By adding a frame, students and teachers can also consider how their strengths will help them achieve their goals. This question is an assets-based reflection, since it assumes that students and teachers have goals. The frame encourages them to consider how their strengths will support them in achieving their goals.
- **To develop a composite of strengths.** Students can begin working in pairs, then larger groups, until they have identified, recorded, and tallied all of the class, grade, or school strengths. When the school posted bulletin boards outside every classroom for Back to School Night to capture the strengths of each class, one class decided to create a display entitled "Our Universe of Strengths." Each strength was written on a star. The stars varied in size depending upon the

number of class members who identified that quality as a strength.

- **To identify and celebrate diverse strengths.** In addition to making composites, students can employ another set of cognitive processing skills by conducting some comparisons, such as comparing student strengths to teacher strengths, or one grade level's strengths to another.

Strengths Walks

In addition to having family members read the bulletin boards, some schools plan Strengths Walks. Students visit with their partner classrooms to review the strengths display and comment on what they see.

Visitors are put together into several groups and guided to do one of the following tasks: look for patterns, comment on the positive aspects of the display, point out what they find surprising, ask questions, provide "I wonder" comments, and so on. After looking over the display and discussing their findings, students write down their observations and comments on different colored post-its, which they then add to the display.

All About Me Tree Map

A group of educators wanted a quick and easy way to get to know their students, uncover student strengths, and build student-to-student relationships. Working together, they came up with the following series of activities to use as an opening year activity.

1. Working individually, each student created a Tree Map, one of the Thinking Maps (Hyerle, 2004), entitled All About Me.

2. Working in pairs, students compared their responses, first looking at their similarities and then their differences.

3. Working in pairs students probed further, responding to the following prompt: What are you dying to ask your partner?

4. Working individually students completed the following writing frame that they shared with their partner (based upon the work of Rothstein, Rothstein & Lauber, 2007):

- I discovered some wonderful things about _____
  _____.
- First, I discovered _____
  _____.
- I also discovered _____
  _____.
- Finally, I discovered _____
  _____.

This activity offers students multiple ways to highlight their strengths and values. This provides teachers with a wellspring of information on what is relevant and meaningful to their students as well as cultural information that teachers can use to further engage students and find ways to validate who they are.

FIGURE 3: **All About Me Tree Map**

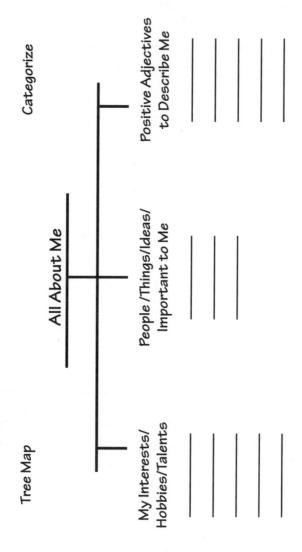

Identifying and Activating Strengths Throughout the Year

Deliberately seeking out ways to activate strengths throughout the year is a culture changer. Here are several suggestions for weaving a strengths-based focus into the fabric of the school year.

Strengths Celebrations

Teachers in the Buffalo, New York public schools face an ongoing uphill battle. For a complicated set of reasons, the school system has been labeled as "failing" for many years. Not surprisingly, morale is low. After participating in professional learning experiences on starting from student strengths, teachers in several Buffalo Public Schools began the exciting, perspective-changing, and spirit-lifting journey to reframe their viewpoint of their students and schools.

Two days after participating in a professional learning experience that focused on identifying and activating student strengths, one group of teachers was so taken by the idea of a strengths focus that they planned and executed a school-wide strengths celebration. It was also the end of the year, just before testing, when anxiety levels are up and end-of-year fatigue has set in.

All of the adults in the building from the principal to the cafeteria workers wrote down an adjective that completed this sentence stem: *You are built to be . . .* Everyone was photographed holding up a placard with that person's chosen word, such as capable, successful, witty, artistic, independent, courageous, and savvy. The photos were put together into a montage accompanied by the song "Dream" by Miley Cyrus. The film was shown at a test prep rally to a cheering student body, and again at the 8th grade moving up ceremony.

Strengths Hunts

Strengths hunts can take many forms. One way is to have students think of a time when they succeeded in achieving a goal or recount a person in history, their family, or the media who succeeded in achieving a goal. The key is to help them uncover and name the skills, attitudes, or behaviors that led to success.

Habits of Mind are the attributes people display when they are acting intelligently (Costa & Kallick, 2000). Ron Ritchhart describes dispositions as overarching sets of acquired patterns of behavior that one controls and deploys fluidly in highly contextualized situations (2002). Often students can use some help labeling these characteristics. Teachers find that building a discussion around the 16 Habits of Mind and intellectual dispositions provides students with a ready-made supply of vocabulary words and concepts that describe effective actions, cognitive processes, and life skills that foster productive problem-solving, decision-making, and communication skills.

Welcoming New Students with Alliterative Introductions

Many teachers use Alliterative Introductions whenever a new student arrives in class as a way of helping a new student integrate seamlessly into a new learning environment. For an added challenge, many teachers tell their students that they cannot use the same adjective they previously used to introduce themselves.

Post-It Affirmations

Establishing rituals that highlight strengths is another ongoing activity to ensure that students reflect often about assets. One ritual we use at the end of workshop sessions— which many teachers have adapted to the classroom—is to have partners write down on a post-it a strength that they observed their partner demonstrate during the session. We ask partners to share their observations and then give the post-it to their partners to keep in their notebooks as a way of reminding them that they possess strengths. Used periodically throughout the year, the collection of post-its continually grows, providing a record of strengths, ongoing affirmation of assets, and a constant reminder that everyone has strengths that should be noted and celebrated.

Strengths Portfolios

Some of the best portfolios are those that students compile and annotate reflectively. Providing time for students to develop and maintain a Strengths Portfolio is a powerful way to highlight strengths development as a key aspect of your class culture and a focus of your students' development. All of the suggested activities in this section can be maintained in a Strengths Portfolio. But it need not end with these activities.

Portfolios foster student engagement and open up a space for student creativity and personalization. In other words, a Strengths Portfolio can be a reflection of student strengths. Artistic students can add artwork. Writers can genre switch, such as converting prose to poetry. The students who are gamers can create a strengths game. The mathematicians in the class can devise "strengths formulas." The scientists can research the neurobiology of strengths. Digitally savvy students can create electronic portfolios, videos, blogs, multimedia presentations, and websites that explore various aspects of strengths.

Mediating Learning to Develop Academic Strengths

Joseph Renzulli's research of individuals labeled as "gifted" illustrates how strengths are developed. He has identified three common traits among these individuals: above average ability, task commitment, and creativity. "However (and this is key to his research), he discovered that these three traits were not manifested in everything gifted individuals did, but rather appeared in relation to things that they had a passionate interest in—interest that when guided evolved into exceptional strengths or 'gifts'" (Jackson, 2011, p. 25).

Students develop and manifest strengths in academics in much the same way: when teachers use strategies and opportunities that bridge learning to their interests and abilities—their cultural frames of reference. By culture we mean what is relevant and meaningful to students. This cultural connection is the missing link for many students in school. Some might argue that this omission is not by accident. Yet teachers who deliberately tap into students' culture tap into a treasure trove of strengths, and in doing so, they set up students for academic acceleration. This deliberate intervention is called *mediation*, the intentional transformation of the learning environment to make it more effective for the learner (Feuerstein, 1979). Teachers who employ youth culture as a bridge to academic learning do so because they see youth culture as a strength, not an impediment, and the results are often staggering (Duncan-Andrade & Morrell, 2008; Mahiri, 1998).

Bridging to students' cultural frames of reference primes students for engagement and is the platform for identifying and activating academic strengths. These strengths are exhibited through teaching strategies to "elicit gifted behaviors and habits of mind, expose students to content that builds their frames of reference and engages exploration, support development of the requisite skills to strengthen cognition and enable self-directed learning, and provide opportunities for the application of interests and learning in authentic and meaningful ways" (Jackson, 2011, p. 25).

Priming: Using Students' Cultural Concepts

Often teachers begin a unit or a lesson by eliciting what students know about a topic or subject. We have found that broadening this initial exploration to find out what students know about an underlying concept is a much richer, and strength-based, approach to priming.

For example, beginning a unit on the civil rights movement by asking students to recall what they know about civil rights rewards those students who possess prior knowledge about this particular topic. Starting with a concept familiar to all students, such as equality, broadens the discussion to include all students' cultural references and unique sets of experiences. (A concept is the term that identifies what you want students to understand is behind the topic. In the case of the civil rights movement, the concepts include understandings such as response to equality, freedom, or oppression.) It is not difficult to get students to explain how their particular experience or example ties into a broader concept. The kind of thinking they do in explicating the connection provides them with an opportunity to do critical analysis, comparative thinking, or evaluation with critique, all cognitive functions assessed in the Common Core State Standards.

School as Cultural Mirror

One of the most powerful ways to cultivate and amplify students' academic strengths is to ensure that students see themselves reflected positively in the curriculum, on bulletin boards and displays, and at institutionalized events and celebrations; in other words, in all aspects of school life. This takes conscious attention and effort, especially if a school is new to this orientation.

Schools can begin with a cultural audit. Get a team of people together. Feel free to include students, family members, and community members. Peruse a school text. Look at a hall display. Observe a school event. Answer these simple questions:

- Who is represented?
- Who is missing?
- Whose voices are heard?
- Whose voices are silenced?

Then ask the following:

- Do those represented and those whose voices are heard reflect the demographic makeup of the school?
- Are various genders represented? Abled and disabled? Children of color and 'white?' Native English speakers and non-native English speakers? Economically advantaged and economically challenged?

These questions and the patterns that emerge will provide some insight into the extent to which your school is providing opportunities for students to see themselves reflected positively in the daily life of the school.

Curriculum as Window and Mirror

Culturally Relevant Teaching is teaching that incorporates students' background knowledge and prior home and community experiences into curriculum and learning experiences (Ladson-Billings, 1994). One powerful and simple way of opening up a space for students to recognize and reflect upon their lived experiences is to use a text processing strategy we call Window Mirror, which is based upon the work of Emily Style (1988), who introduced the concept of curriculum as window and mirror. By this, she means that some aspects of curriculum constitute a window into other worlds, while other aspects are mirrors of a student's culture, background, experiences, and values.

As students read a text, they mark with a *W* any aspect of the text that is a window for them. Similarly, they mark with an *M* any aspect of the text that is a mirror for them. After a period of reading time in which students read and mark up the text, they share their annotations with a partner or a small group.

By explicitly asking students to look for ways in which the text reflects them, it validates and affirms their cultural capital. In other words, this activity sends a message that where they come from, how they see the world, and what resonates with them has merit. It also highlights the notion that there is more than one way to see the world.

Give One, Get One

Use a cooperative learning strategy such as Give One, Get One to address content and assessment through a strengths lens. This simple process can be used at any grade level in any content area as a powerful strengths-based rehearsal and review of content, concepts, and processes.

1. Students jot down three things they know about the assigned topic, concept, or process. (The number can be increased for older students.)

2. At a signal, students move around the room and find a partner. Partners exchange one of their responses that their partner does not have. Their partner records that response in the Get One column.

3. This process is repeated until all students have given three things and received three things.

When kindergarten students record in words or graphically represent three things they know about flowers, or when high school social studies students jot down in words or graphically represent three key ideas on how economic decision making has become global as a result of an interdependent world economy, they are starting their review from an assets base. They are recording what they know using a medium (words or graphics) that is part of their strengths repertoire. Explaining orally what they have recorded reinforces what they know and builds their vocabulary. Recording what their fellow students know and understand about a topic serves as a further review.

An Array of Ways to Activate Strengths

Encouraging students to express themselves through nontraditional means gives them an opportunity to tap into their strengths, often representative of their out-of-school interests. Since these opportunities require students to convert academic learning into another form, they employ comparative thinking, critical analysis, synthesis, and conceptualization as they communicate their understandings and interpretations in an alternate form.

We have found that successful alternative means of demonstrating knowledge share certain characteristics: They work best at the end of lesson or unit to capture essential understandings; they are conducted in a joyful, playful manner; students work in pairs or small groups; students have specific directions about the kind and amount of content to be included (at least three facts, essential characteristics of, etc.); tasks are switched up throughout the year to provide novelty; students are given a brief time limit in which to come up with their final product; whatever is created is shared—and applauded.

Here are some of our favorite alternative ways of demonstrating cognitive and knowledge strength:

- **Genre Switching** converts one form of expression into another. For example, a historical event is rewritten as a poem or newspaper article or represented as a political cartoon. Nonfiction, explanatory text can be transformed into a Reader's Theater script.
- **Nonverbal Representations** allow students to employ their visualization and graphic arts abilities to capture essential elements of concepts or topics under study. This strategy demonstrates students' ability to critically analyze conceptual understanding. We love to use them as a processing tool to summarize a reading, talk, or movie section by section.

- **Symbolic Representations** require students to analyze, synthesize, and demonstrate concepts metaphorically. The quality of the product is often less important than their articulation of what their representation means.
- **Six-Word Stories** are very short stories that literally use no more than six words. They are effective vehicles for summarizing any form of text or any concept drawn from the content areas.
- **Analogies** or comparisons are known to be mind stretchers. We often use a Bridge Map, one of the Thinking Maps (Hyerle, 2004), as a means of developing and deepening a concept. Students asked to consider the concept of oppression came up with the following analogies: Stress oppresses learning as censorship oppresses free expression.
- **Tableaus** allow students to represent an event or concept using a group of motionless figures. Determining how to position each figure and what kind of expressions each figure should wear is highly conceptual and interpretive.
- **Skits** provide students free rein to demonstrate their knowledge through creation of a news broadcast, a talking heads show, a cartoon, a game show, or anything familiar to them. These skits demonstrate students' strengths in conceptualization and language usage.
- **Jingles** shine the spotlight on those students who are wordsmiths, can synthesize and conceptualize, have a sense of patterns, or can create a tune.

- **Slogans** depend upon capturing the essence or conceptual understanding of content, which is often complex, in order to reduce it to something catchy and memorable.
- **Frame of Reference** asks students to analyze a situation through the lens of someone else, thinking dialogically. We ask students to tear out a frame from a piece of blank paper and record reactions from someone else's perspective. Flip the frame over and they can repeat the process from another person's frame of reference. An example is Civil War through the frame of reference of a Buffalo soldier. This demonstrates conceptual understanding and keen emotional intelligence.
- **Graffiti** is part of urban settings and is derived from a long tradition of people marking walls with images and words that capture everyday events, make political statements, or give expression to individual thoughts and feelings. Supplied with markers, butcher paper, and a prompt, students create graffiti walls in which they respond individually using stylized lettering and graphics. After explaining their contributions and looking for themes, they write responses (Allender, 2014). These demonstrate comprehension of events, analysis, attention to details, synthesis, and astute sense of articulating understandings graphically.
- **Poetry** provides more than opportunities for self-expression. Its various forms and styles make it a creative vehicle for students to demonstrate language

usage and critical and analysis of key concepts and ideas that are part of the standard curriculum.

Efforts to highlight strengths come in many forms. For several years, some of the schools labeled as "lowest performing" in the Newark Public Schools participated in StudentVoices NUA projects. One such project involved middle school students producing books with their thoughts on various themes. For example, *The Justice Epistles* (NUA, 2011) gave their takes on justice, including their deep understanding of the world around them and unbounded resiliency in the face of many oppressive, unjust, and often violent situations. In *Go! Put Your Strengths Out There* (NUA, 2009), students reflected upon and gave expression to their strengths in various forms of writing and graphic representations.

One 7th grader clearly gave much thought to his strengths, which he articulated in a three-stanza poem. The first two lines provide a powerful definition of what strengths are. When he says, "Your strengths inhabit the void where your weaknesses struggle," the reader needs to pause. These two opening lines demonstrate a command of language one would not necessarily associate with a student from a "failing" school. The image of strengths residing in a void where weaknesses struggle is powerful, thought-provoking, and deep. He asserts that strengths and weaknesses are closely aligned: They are neighbors, inhabiting the same void.

After reading this definition, it is hard to argue with his assertion that his strength is writing. It is where his intellect clearly shows, he says. And to prove the point the poem continues with powerful words and images chronicling his different strengths. Those who have ever worked through a difficult math problem can see their confusion reflected in his description of numbers and equations, which he describes as toppling through his head. Similarly, we resonate with his sense of euphoria when he solves the problem. To complete the verbal portrait of his strengths, he talks about his forays into sports where, he asserts, failure may be rare, and when it does come, he doubles his efforts spurred by a special kind of determination.

In the final, confidence-infused stanza, he reminds readers that he has many strengths, then he issues a challenge. He essentially says, if you try to get the better of him, you had better think again because his strengths will shine through and you will not beat him.

How wonderful for this student that he believes he cannot be beat. Our role as educators is to make certain all the students we teach can identify their strengths, gloat over them a bit, and assert with confidence that they "can't be beat."

As educators, we have been distracted from identifying and activating student strengths. A relentless focus on weaknesses has not served our students or us well. Through conscious recognition and deliberate practice, however, we can refocus attention on strengths. In strengths-focused classrooms, students are given free rein to hone their abilities to uncover latent strengths, deepen their use of existing strengths, wield their strengths in innovative ways, and develop new strengths. This provides insight to them—and to us—about their innate potential, developing interests, and self-determination. All we have to do is shine the spotlight on strengths—deliberately, consistently, and meaningfully.

ASCD | arias™

ENCORE

IDENTIFYING AND ACTIVATING STRENGTHS CONTINUUM

Having a deliberate and consistent process to determine where a school experience or interaction falls in terms of amplifying or disregarding strengths is key. An example of a simple process is the Identifying and Activating Strengths Continuum, which offers a way to think through a school experience or interaction to

- Recognize whether it leans more heavily toward amplifying or disregarding strengths.
- Reflect on ways in which the experience or interaction could be nudged closer to the goal of amplifying strengths.

The tool is simple enough to use on the fly in response to an observed situation such as a comment overheard or an action observed in passing. It is also robust enough to use in settings such as faculty meetings on more formal aspects of schooling like curriculum, textbook content, and lesson design. For maximum impact, apply this continuum regularly, deliberately, and unapologetically over time.

Sample I: Comments

Michael, a student whose behavior the day before was deemed to cause problems, is greeted by his teacher the next morning: "I trust you're going to have a better day today." This comment falls very far away from the goal of amplifying

Identifying and Activating Strengths Continuum

<--->

Disregards   Amplifies
Strengths   Strengths

this student's strengths. It not only fails to mention any of Michael's strengths, it also draws attention to the teacher's assessment of Michael as a problem.

Alternatively, a greeting that includes words such as the following is welcoming, positive, and strengths amplifying: "So good to see you, Michael. Later we are going to be responding to the story we read yesterday by illustrating the part that resonated with us. I know drawing is your passion and your strength. I cannot wait to see what you draw!"

For Consideration: Where on the continuum would you place the following comment that we often hear applied to underachieving students: "These students come to school without any experiences"? How might you reconceive and reword it to reflect student strengths?

Sample II: Lesson and Assessments

To move lessons and assessments to the next level of practice, analyze the lesson or assessment to determine how you could redesign the activity give students a chance to discover or cultivate their unique gifts, talents, dispositions, and interests.

For Consideration: Analyze a week's worth of lessons or assessments to determine what patterns emerge. What kinds of strengths tend to be required and rewarded? Which strengths are ignored? What is one specific way you could alter your lessons and assessments to enable more students to show their strengths?

Sample III: Official Documents

The wording, length, and tone of official documents, like policy handbooks and codes of conduct, contain powerful messages. Often federal, state, and local mandates and policies govern what is included in these documents. They are frequently written under the guidance of attorneys, whose major interest is in protecting the institution from liability. Counteracting the negative tone that assumes that students and teachers are likely to harass one another or behave inappropriately at school functions may be difficult, but it is not impossible. One way to get a handle on the messages implied in these official documents is to divide the document into sections. Ask groups to review a section looking for supportive, positive, or strengths affirming language. Share.

For Consideration: Discuss ways in which positive messages that amplify strengths could be embedded in or accompany the document.

References

Allender, D. (2014). Applying student strengths through graffiti boards. Presented at the National Urban Alliance for Effective Education Summer Academy, Minneapolis, MN.

Anderson, E. (2005). Strengths-based educating: A concrete way to bring out the best in students—and yourself. *Educational Horizons, 83*(3), 180–189.

Cohen, G. L., Garcia, J., Apfel, N., & Master, A. (2006). Reducing the racial achievement gap: A social-psychological intervention. *Science, 313*(5791), 1307–1310.

Costa, A. L., & Kallick, B. (2000). *Habits of mind: A developmental series.* Alexandria, VA: ASCD.

Costa, A. L., & Kallick, B. (2014). *Dispositions: Reframing teaching and learning.* Thousand Oaks, CA: Corwin Press.

Duncan-Andrade, J. M. R., & Morrell, E. (2008). *The art of critical pedagogy: Possibilities for moving from theory to practice in urban schools.* New York: Peter Lang.

Feuerstein, R. (1979). Cognitive modifiability in retarded adolescents: Effects of instrumental enrichment. *American Journal of Mental Deficiency, 83*(6), 539–550.

Feuerstein, R., Feuerstein, R. S., & Falik, L. H. (2010). *Beyond smarter: Mediated learning and the brain's capacity for change.* New York: Teachers College Press.

Feuerverger, G. (2007). *Teaching, learning, and other miracles.* Rotterdam, Netherlands: Sense Publishers.

Gallup. (2014, December 11). Fall 2014 U.S. overall student poll results. Retrieved from http://www.gallup.com/services/180029/gallup-student-poll-2014-overall-report.aspx

Holloway, M. (2003). The mutable brain. *Scientific American, 289*(3), 79–85.

Hyerle, D. (Ed.). (2004). *Student successes with Thinking Maps: School-based research, results, and models for achievement using visual tools.* Thousand Oaks, CA: Corwin Press.

Jackson, Y. (2011). *The pedagogy of confidence: Inspiring high intellectual performance in urban schools.* New York: Teachers College Press.

Jackson, Y., & McDermott, V. (2012). *Aim high, achieve more: How to transform urban schools through fearless leadership*. Alexandria, VA: ASCD.

Jensen, E. (1998). *Teaching with the brain in mind*. Alexandria, VA: ASCD.

Jensen, E. (2005). *Teaching with the brain in mind* (2nd ed.). Alexandria, VA: ASCD.

Ladson-Billings, G. (1994). *The dreamkeepers: Successful teachers of African American children*. San Francisco, CA: Jossey-Bass.

Mahiri, J. (1998). *Shooting for excellence: African American and youth culture in new century schools*. Urbana, IL: National Council of Teachers of English; New York: Teachers College Press.

McDermott, V. (2010). Student radio: Magnifying voices, preparing a future. *ASCD Express, 5*(22).

National Governors Association Center for Best Practices & Council of Chief State School Officers. (2010). *Common Core State Standards*. Washington, DC: Author.

Rath, T., & Conchie, B. (2008). *Strengths based leadership: Great leaders, teams, and why people follow*. New York: Gallup Press.

Renzulli, J. S. (1975). Talent potential in minority group students. In W. Barbe & J. Renzulli (Eds.), *Psychology and education of the gifted*. New York: Irvington.

Renzulli, J. S. (1978). What makes giftedness? Reexamining a definition. *Phi Delta Kappan, 60*(3), 180–184.

Renzulli, J. S. (1998). The three-ring conception of giftedness. In S. M. Baum, S. M. Reis, & L.R. Maxfield. (Eds.), *Nurturing the gifts and talents of primary grade students*. Mansfield Center, CT: Creative Learning Press.

Renzulli, J. S., & Reis, S. M. (2007). A technology based program that matches enrichment resources with student strengths, *iJET International Journal of Emerging Technologies in Learning, 3*(2).

Ritchhart, R. (2002). *Intellectual character: What it is, why it matters, and how to get it*. San Francisco, CA: Jossey-Bass.

Rothstein, A., Rothstein, E. & Lauber, G. (2007). *Writing as learning: A content-based approach* (2nd ed.). Thousand Oaks, CA: Corwin Press.

Steele, C., & Aronson, J. (2004). The stereotype threat. Retrieved from http://www.mtholyoke.edu/offices/comm/csj/092404/steele.shtml

Style, E. (1988). Curriculum as window and mirror. *Listening for all the voices*. Oak Knoll School Monograph. Summit, NJ.

Related Resources

At the time of publication, the following ASCD resources were available (ASCD stock numbers appear in parentheses). For up-to-date information about ASCD resources, go to www.ascd.org. You can search the complete archives of *Educational Leadership* at http://www.ascd.org/el.

ASCD EDge®
Exchange ideas and connect with other educators interested in various topics, including strengths-based teaching, on the social networking site ASCD EDge at http://ascdedge.ascd.org.

Print Products
Aim High, Achieve More: How to Transform Urban Schools Through Fearless Leadership by Yvette Jackson and Veronica McDermott (#112015)

The Differentiated Classroom: Responding to the Needs of All Learners, 2nd Edition by Carol Ann Tomlinson (#108029)

Engaging Students with Poverty in Mind: Practical Strategies for Raising Achievement by Eric Jensen (#113001)

Fostering Grit: How Do I Prepare My Students for the Real World? (ASCD Arias) by Thomas R. Hoerr (#SF113075)

ASCD PD Online® Courses
Understanding Student Motivation, 2nd edition (#PD11OC106)
This and other online courses are available at www.ascd.org/pdonline.

DVDs
Engaging Students with Poverty in Mind DVD series (#613041)
A Visit to a Motivated Classroom (#603384)

For more information: send e-mail to member@ascd.org; call 1-800-933-2723 or 703-578-9600, press 2; send a fax to 703-575-5400; or write to Information Services, ASCD, 1703 N. Beauregard St., Alexandria, VA 22311-1714 USA.

About the Authors

 **Yvette Jackson** currently serves as the Chief Executive Officer of the National Urban Alliance for Effective Education. She is the author of the 2011 ForeWord Reviews' Silver Book of the Year Award, *The Pedagogy of Confidence: Inspiring High Intellectual Performance in Urban Schools*, and co-author with Veronica McDermott of *Aim High, Achieve More: How to Transform Urban Schools Through Fearless Leadership*.

 **Veronica McDermott** is a lifelong educator and passionate ally in the cause of social justice, whose legacy project is to eradicate the crime of squandered potential.